LATER FOR YOU

2007- 2008

STEPHANIE JACOBSON

© 2010 by Sugar Doll Publishing
All rights reserved.
ISBN 978-0-9833961-3-0

Printed in the United States of America.

Table of Contents

THIS MAGNIFICENT HUNGER	3
MY FEAST	4
DANCE IN THE FLAMES	5
BOUND	6
JOIN ME	7
ONE LAST PROMISE	8
DAZZLE ME	9
THIS MORNING	10
CONTROL	11
DRINK	12
TOO DAMN HIGH	13
LONG TIME, NO SEE	14
TO DO	15
20/20	16
SPARK	17
A MOMENT	18
WHOLE NEW WAY	19
TIME TO TIME	20
SHE	21
CAN'T WAIT	22
I GET IT	23
PASSAGE OF TIME	24
MILLION AND ONE	25
STRUNG TOGETHER	26
COMFORTABLY NUMB	27
JEKYLL AND HYDE	28
JUST A WAY	29
MASTERPIECE	30
GO BACK	31
GROWS COLDER	32
DO NOT WANT	33
SOMETHING MORE	34
CAUGHT IN MY NET	35
I WRITE	36
BAD DAY	37
DO YOU REMEMBER?	38
BEFORE	39

Table of Contents

TIME	40
INSTANT	41
SEE?	42
SUNDAY MORNING	43
FINISH LINE	44
ENVIOUS	45
OWES YOU	46
QUIET TIME	47
TOO MUCH TIME	48
AFTERNOON NAPS	49
BOTH SIDES	50
ALL FIGURED OUT	51
HIS HAPPINESS	52
BACK TO WORK	53
FIRST DATE	54
FIFTEEN YEARS	55
REINVENTION	56
PLAYING CATCH UP	58
I AM	59
AFTERNOON	60
TO DO LIST	61
MEANS TO AN END	62
CONNECTION	63
PROTEST	64
REMEMBER?	65
A WRITER	66
PAVLOV	67
JUST DINNER	68
SNAP	69
APOLOGIES	70
RIGHT THING	71
TIME	72
IF I…	73
MIDNIGHT	74
YOU	75
LEFT OFF	76
MONKEY POEMS	77

Table of Contents

MONKEY WRITES A POEM	78
SHARING A HOME	79
ANTICIPATION	81
FRAME BY FRAME	81
MORNING	82
MIDDLE OF A DREAM	84
WHAT WAS	86
WRITING TO FIND	88
SAID IT BETTER	89
GREAT POETRY READING DAY	90
YOUR HEARTBEAT	91
DEAL	92
SOMETHING WITH YOU	93
DAY OF THE YEAR	95
I REMEMBER	96
BITCH	97
TURN BACK TIME	98
GET LOST	99
IT'S THE WAY	101
FACT OR FICTION	102
TUCK AND ROLL	103
A TOAST	104
RULES	105
FREE FORM	106
CALL ME BABY	108
KER-PLOOEY	109
DANCERS	110
CROSSROADS	111
ALWAYS A WAY	112
HAD TO DO	112
RAIN	112
IDEAL STANDARDS	112
SECOND CHANCE	113
UNFINISHED	113
TRUST	113
REGRET	113
IN BED	114
WHERE YOU'VE BEEN	114

this magnificent hunger

This magnificent hunger
I ache to devour
Want to kiss sugar skin
Your haunting gaze
My desire burns
The whisper of a dream
A fevered fire fantasy
Too beautiful for words

my feast

I draw a breath
Ragged
As you stir my soul
Ravaged
I am hungry and
You are my feast
Laid out before me
My gift cleverly wrapped
In the guise of a dream
I reach out to touch you
Far away, so close
My fingers dance
Across the soft skin
That trembles beneath the touch

dance in the flames

Night lingers and
I long for your
Fevered embrace
To dance in the flames
Of passion

bound

I want you naked
And waiting in my bed
Hands bound to the
Bed posts
Waiting for me
To do with you
As I please

join me

Whisper to me
A sacred song
That I've never known
A tantalizing embrace
Drenched in passion
Devoured in fevered hunger
Exploring this delicious caress
Every movement in harmony
Join me in this dance

one last promise

My heart broke
When I said goodbye to you
My heart
My soul
My love
But all good things
Must come to an end
Or so I'm told
Pleasantries
Exchanged
And wishing well
And one last promise
That I'll always be here
And it was over
Just like that
No turning back now
It was time to explore
The world alone
Seek refuge in another's arms
And hope it can live up
To the expectations
Placed upon it
By the years I spent with you

dazzle me

Dazzle me with
Your brilliant rhythm
Of music composed
With abstract passion
In a delicious dream

this morning

I wake up
Curled around your warm body
And snuggle back into bed
Not wanting to lose this moment
I have nowhere else to be
This morning
Than right here next to you
I love watching you sleep
So peaceful and content
Blissfully unaware of my gaze
As I take in the sight before me

control

When I first started threatening
To tie you to the bed
And have my way with you
I meant it as a joke
But here you are
Naked and handcuffed
To a hotel bed
At my mercy
"I never pegged you as
The submissive type"
I say, lighting the candle and
Waiting for the wax to pool
"I wouldn't be here if I didn't
Want to be"
You answer, clearly the one
Who's really in control

drink

Drink like your life depends on it
And all of your problems will be solved
Isn't that the way it works
In your world?
Raise your glass in a toast
And fuck the rest
It's their problem
Not yours
Isn't that right?

too damn high

I have nothing
More to offer you
That I haven't already given
I've offered up everything
Still you ask for more
Are you disappointed?
Did I let you down?
Or are your expectations
Just too damn high?

long time, no see

Man, it's good to see you again
Almost too good
As the memories of the times we shared
All come rushing back to me
And for a moment
I think
Letting you go
Could have been a mistake
I quickly push those thoughts aside
As I pour you a cup of coffee
And sit down across from you
To get caught up on all the things
We've missed out on
You come to me
New and reinvented
And I can't help but think
What if we'd stayed together?
I would've missed out
On my second chance at love
And waking up
To those beautiful brown eyes
Smiling back at me
And a love I never thought
I'd have again

to do

There's so much to do
Such little time to do it
Isn't that what they all say?
I find that if I really
Buckle down
And get to it
I can get it all done
Instead I procrastinate
Then bitch when I run out of time

20/20

They say hindsight
Is always twenty-twenty
And I guess that's true
I didn't realize how much
We were holding each other
Down
Until I let go
It wasn't easy
But I had to do it
And now I think
Leaving you
Was the best thing
I could have done
For us

spark

What sparks creativity?
A word?
A picture?
A song?
A moment?
I suppose it could be anything
But if that's the case
Why is it so hard
For me to write anything?

a moment

It only took a moment
The right moment
For me to fall
Under your spell
Your simple whispered words
Fell like a symphony
On my ears
And somewhere between
The night and the morning
And waking from my dreams
I find you here
Next to me
Like it was always meant to be

whole new way

Let me introduce you
To a life you never knew
A raw and simple pleasure
You've never experienced
Let me show you a whole new way
To experience life and love
We could be tremendous together
Given the chance

time to time

How would things be different
If you never woke up this morning
Or any of the mornings before?
I still think about it
From time to time
But you'd never know that
Even if you asked
I'd never tell you
It would cause more problems
Than it would be worth
I'd never expect you to understand
anyway

she

she's trying to balance
the good girl with the bad
the life of the party
with the life-giving mother
she fights so hard
to be everything to everyone
and in the meantime
loses herself
and who she really is
she's still trying to figure out
what she wants to be
when she grows up

she's afraid of changing
but afraid of staying the same
trying to be a chameleon
blending in with her surroundings
not wanting to be the outsider
she always has been
so she tries to balance
who she is
with who she wants to be
hoping she can fool some of them
at least some of the time

can't wait

I have vowed to write
A poem a day
Thinking it would be easy
I used to do it all the time
But that was many years ago
Before all of the
Responsibilities
And time-consuming chores
That make up day-to-day adulthood
It's funny how when we're young
We can't wait to grow up
And once we've grown up
We wish things could be more like
childhood

i get it

Okay
Enough
I get it
You ain't got time for me
And my middle-class
Stay at home mom mediocrity
So I'll just sit here waiting
For you to throw me some scraps
Of your flashy
High-flying falsehood
Of security

passage of time

It's almost three a.m.
And I'm sitting here
Unaware
Of the passage of time
Through the revolving door
Of missed opportunities
And unanswered calls

million and one

I've got a million and one things
That I need to do
And a million and one reasons
To not do them
Procrastination is an art
Which I've studied for years
And practice makes perfect
Or so they say

strung together

It's a stream of
Consciousness
That keeps my pen to page
Writing down the words
Before they disappear
It keeps me up
Late at night
Afraid to miss a moment
Of supposed brilliance
It's kind of like thinking everything you say
Is brilliant when you're drunk
And in the hazy details
Of the morning after
You realize it just
Words on a page
Sure, they sounded pretty
Under the influence
But in the stone-sober light of reality
They're just big, pretty words
Not so cleverly strung together

comfortably numb

There were so many reasons
Why I should have walked away
But there were too many lies
And just as many last times
All of which just made me want to stay
Grasping at straws
And lapping up the crumbs
Of hope long ago shattered
Why start over
Somewhere new
When I'm comfortably numb with you?

jekyll and hide

The sound of ice
Clinking in your glass
Is the only warning signal
I have
Of a night soon to be filled
With words that cannot be
Taken back
One after another
You drink them down
Becoming less and less
Like the person I love
And more and more
The person I loathe
It's your doctor Jekyll
And mister Hyde
And in the light of the morning
You'll forget every word
You said to me

just a way

You ask me if I love you
Or if you're just a way
To pass the time
And you're bothered by
How long it takes
For me to answer

masterpiece

I'm trying desperately
To not end up writing
Something silly and trite
But maybe that's the way to go?
I mean,
We can't be serious all of the time
So why do I feel everything
Has to be thought provoking
Or tugging at the heartstrings?
They don't all have to be
Masterpieces
Hell, they don't even have to be good
They just have to be
Just existing to exist

go back

I feel as if
Some of my best work
Is already behind me
And all I'm doing
Is trying to
Recapture
What I've already lost
Whether it be a word
Or a phrase
Or a precise moment in time
It's all behind me now
And when I look ahead
All I see is
Someone trying to go back

grows colder

I light another cigarette
And grab my pen
Find a clean sheet of paper
And write
I get a few words down
Before inspiration
Drifts away
And I take a sip
Of my lukewarm coffee
While I wait for it to return
My cigarette
Slowly burns
In the ashtray
I only lit it out of habit
Anyway
Taking a drag
Again grabbing my pen
And scribbling down
A few lines of fleeting words
And my coffee grows colder

do not want

I do not want
This
Empty feeling of
Worthlessness
But it seems
No matter what
I do
To chase it away
I only seem
To bring it closer

something more

If I keep
Holding out
For something more
I'll miss all of
The great opportunities
Being presented to me
In the moment
Don't waste all of your
Goodbyes on me
I'm not the one
Who chose to do the
Leaving
So just go ahead
And walk away
Just make sure you turn your back on me
When you do
I don't want you to
See me crying
Over losing you

caught in my net

All of these thoughts
Swirling around in my head
Yet I can't seem to form them
Into any sense
Of cohesiveness
They flutter around
Like butterflies
Twirling and dancing
And refusing to be
Caught in my net

i write

I write
In hopes that
My words
Spark
Something inside of someone

I write
To get
It all out
Of my head
Whatever is going on
In there

I write
For I am
A writer

And in the end
I write
For me and
No one else
So do with these words
What you will
Because I,
The writer,
Will just keep writing

bad day

She lashes out
For no particular reason
At whoever is around
Taking it all out
On innocent bystanders
And when the smoke
Finally clears
She's surprised to see
There's no one left standing there

do you remember

Do you remember
The first time
I tried to kiss you?
I can imagine
Why you wouldn't
You were standing there
Fumbling through your bag
Trying to find a shirt
And I stood there
Watching you
I was outwardly calm and cool
And inwardly nervous
About what I was about to do
I had planned on kissing you
That night
You tried in vain to
Seem disinterested in me
And my not-so-subtle advances
As I handed you your shirt
Which had fallen on the floor
Unbuckled your belt
Unzipped your jeans
And let my fingers dance
Across you
But
Your tilted head
Closed eyes
And parted lips
Gave you away
Yes, I planned on
Kissing you that night
But I didn't
I couldn't
I wasn't willing to break the spell
That had been cast upon us
So I kissed the top of your head
Ruffled your hair
And walked out of the room

before

You were the one
Who had done this before
Sensing your nervousness
Wasn't really helpful
But it was oddly comforting
As I blindly put my
Trust into your capable hands

time

Time waits for
No man
But I wish it would
Wait for me
Seems I've bitten off
More than I can
Chew again
And now I'm burning the
Candle at both ends
Trying to get everything done

instant

In this world of
Instant
Gratification
My patience is
Being stretched
Thin by having to
Wait

see?

I light another cigarette
Take a sip of wine and
Change the song that's playing
I'm looking for something
That will stir inside of me
Bring up something
Anything
To keep me going
Keep me writing
Even if
All I end up writing is crap
I'm not looking to be
The next big thing
To the written word
My ambitions have never been that lofty
I just want something to show
Something that says
See?
I wasn't really wasting
My time
When I sat there staring
At a blank page
For hours
Neglecting everything else around me

sunday morning

Reluctantly
I drag myself out
Of your bed
And make my way
To the kitchen
I open the cupboard
Pull down your favorite coffee mug
And pour in the coffee
A little bit of sugar
And that chocolate-caramel creamer you like
The same way
I've watched you make you coffee
Many mornings before this one
Quickly
I head back upstairs
Where you're waiting for me
Still snuggled
In the covers and pillows
You roll over
Sit up
And I hand you your coffee
And snuggle myself back in
Every other Sunday morning
This is our routine
A routine I miss
When I'm not here with you

finish line

The faster I run
To the finish
Line
The further away
It gets
At least that's how it seems

When I was
Younger
I used to have this dream
You know the ones where you're being chased
By some unknown thing
You run and run
You can see your way of escape ahead of you
But it never seems to get any closer
Yet the foot steps behind you
Fall louder
Faster
Heavier

I never found out how
That dream ended
That was usually the point when i
Woke up
In a cold sweat
Heart leaping from my chest

envious

I am slightly
Envious
Of the people who can
Sit down
And write these long poems
The ability to take
Average
Every day words
And string them together
Into beautiful prose
With meaning, no less
With purpose
While I just struggle
To get a few random words
Onto a piece of paper
And I find myself
Trying too hard
And sounding pretentious
Neither of which I want to be

owes you

You think that the world owes you
For something
You haven't even done
Instead of bitching about
What you should have
Get up off your ass
And go get it yourself

quiet time

My quiet time comes
Around two in the morning
When everyone else is asleep
I know I should be
Sleeping too
But I need my quiet time
So I take it whenever I get it
And hope to make the
Most of it
By getting as much done as I can
Before I force myself into bed

too much time

When did you stop dreaming, girl
Accepting things as they are
Becoming complacent
And dare I say dull?
You used to have goals and
Ambition
Now getting out of bed in the morning
Is a big accomplishment for you
You need to shake yourself
Free
From your day-to-day existence
Take a deep breath
And dive into the unknown
Liven it up a bit, baby
You're spending way too much time alone

afternoon naps

It's the little things in life
That make us happy
Isn't it?
Like that forty-five minute nap
Snuck in on a lazy afternoon
The two of us snuggled in
That little cocoon of bliss
I've become accustomed to
That sleepy smile I'm greeted
With before you roll out of bed
You ask if I slept at all
I lie and say I did
When in actuality
I was happy just to lay there
With your head on my chest
Watching you sleep

both sides

I'm running out of patience
For you and your little games
You straddle both sides of
the fence
So you don't have to go far to
Change your point of view
When are you going to learn
That you can't have it both ways?

all figured out

Just when I think I have it
All figured out
They go and change the damn
Rules again
Do this, don't do that
No, wait, do that instead

his happiness

I should be mad at you
For walking in and stealing away
One of the best things that had ever
Happened to me
In the last fifteen years
But I'm not
Something inside of me
Breathed a sigh of relief
When he told me he wanted
To see where you might lead him
It meant no more arguments
No more letting him down
No more disappointment
Of course
It also meant
No more curling up in his arms at night
No more little love notes
Tucked away in my luggage
No more valentines
Those things would all be yours now
But I'm okay with that
Because in the end
The thing that makes me happiest
Is his happiness
And it's clear to me
And everyone else
That you make him happy

back to work

So many things to do
So few people to do them for me
Although if I left
Half of this to the hands of other
It would just create more work
For myself in the end
Since surely they couldn't do it
Quiet like I'd want them to
It would be more
Editing and revision
On top of what I already
Have to do
So I guess I'm left to
Suck it up
Buckle down
And get back to work

first date

You were nervous
Hell, so was I
But I was trying not to show it
Sitting there watching you
Feigning interest in the dessert menu
While you waited for me to make the next move
You're cute when you're nervous
And trying a bit too hard
Probably part of the reason
I became so smitten with you in the first place
The waitress took our orders and
I tried my best to put your mind at ease
Had I not been so determined
To see if you wanted the same thing I did
It probably would've dawned on me sooner
That we were actually on our first date
But I didn't have time to think of things in that light
I just needed to see if we were on the same page
See if this thing was going to go anywhere
So when you leaned over
And kissed me in my car
I was pleasantly surprised
Guess we were on the same page
After all

fifteen years

Fifteen years
Quickly packed away to forget about
Just because you smiled at me
I was instantly hooked
And ready to move on with you
And move away from
The one constant in my life
For the past fifteen years
We said all of the right things
To each other
The 'you'll always be a part of my life'
The 'you're still my friend'
The 'I'm always here for you'
And with a kiss
That might as well have been a handshake
It was over
And I was off to find you
And your smile
Hoping that smile would soon be meant
For me
And me only

reinvention

Every cigarette I light
is one I do not want
But I light it anyway
I think I fear quitting
Because it's like losing a part
of my identity
Not that it's a good part
But it's part of who I am

Then again
I'm in that period of my life
Where I need to reinvent myself
Not totally, just slightly
So maybe it's a good thing
Losing a part of who I am

Then again
If I knew who I really was
There wouldn't be this need
For reinvention
All of the time
I'm coming up on thirty and
I still don't know
what I want to be when I grow up
Sometimes I think it's because my life
lacks direction
But then again
I could change direction at any time
And not screw up
the balance of things in my world
So maybe it's a good thing
Not knowing who you are

I've had people tell me I'm like a chameleon
Always changing
I usually respond with something about
Keeping everybody on their toes
I do it so things don't get stagnant

Cuz who wants to be stuck
doing the same thing
Day in and day out?

I used to look
at milestone birthdays as some
Magic number or something
Like being one year older
would magically change things
That this would be the year
where I finally get it
All of the time
spent trying to figure things out
Would all come together and
Viola!
Now I look at birthdays
as just another day

I should really quit smoking though

playing catch-up

I'm trying to play catch-up
Hoping to somehow come up with
Over five-thousand words
Of poetry
In a week
A week!
A deadline is a funny thing
It's supposed to keep us moving
Keep us motivated
Give us something to look forward to
A finish line to cross
But when you're behind
And that deadline is fast approaching
It's scary, man!
You sit and think about the days that have past
When you should have been working
But weren't
And screaming at yourself for wasting time
You have a deadline to meet!
Get to work!
But when that deadline is far away
You always think you'll have time to make up
The difference
Until it's too late
And you're scrambling to play catch-up

i am

I am
Three hundred
Ninety seven days
Away from
Being thirty years old
Thirty two days
Away from being
Twenty nine
And
Four thousand and
Forty seven days
Away from being
Forty
Some people cringe at the
Passage of time
Like a number means anything
But a number
I've been looking forward to
Thirty
Since twenty five
(Which was one thousand
Seven hundred
Ninety three days ago)
For some reason I feel like
I'll have finally come into my own
At thirty
Like I'm really an adult

afternoon

Birds bob about in the back yard
Picking through the grass
For leftover seeds
Or maybe a worm or two
The cats sit in the window
With chattered meows
The natural instinct to stalk
The sky is gray and looks
Like it could rain any moment
As nice as the sunshine has been
There's nothing nicer
Than a spring rain shower
Curling up on the couch
Listening to the patter of raindrops
Outside the window
The sound calming and refreshing

to do list

She looks around the room
At the many things she has to do
Sips at her coffee and
Does her best Scarlett O'Hara
'After all, tomorrow is another day'

means to an end

Some suicides are never recorded
Because they're not recognized
As suicides
A one car crash on a back road
A tragic accident around the house when no one else was home
An accidental overdose
An unfortunate drowning
Yes, these things all could be
Accidents
Mistakes
Or bad luck
But they could also be
Well thought out
Means to an end

connection

There is no connection
Between what I say and what I do
I talk a big game
I know
But if you pay attention to my actions
You'll know it's all bullshit

protest

I want to write a protest poem
But I'm not sure how to
Go about doing so
I want to protect my freedom of speech
And your freedom of religion
I want a say
In who I should be able to to marry
Be it a man or a woman
I want to be able to shout
It's my body to do with as I please
And talk about how the oil companies are
Raping the country by charging $3.70 a gallon
A paycheck barely covers the gas needed to get to a job
Where you're already underpaid
I want to ask how much longer
Are we going to let our sons and daughters suffer fighting a war
Yet how we forget about our children at home
Who take guns to school to solve their problems
Yes, I want to write a protest poem
But I'm not sure how to

remember?

I have this sea foam green
Cowl neck sweater
That's ruined
Due to a red stain across the collar
After spending the night
In the bathroom
At the bar
Throwing up
After god knows how many drinks
(Nobody kept count…obviously)
And most of that night is a blur
I do know that I was carried out of the bar
Something I've never had happen before
Kele drove me home
And I crawled across my front lawn
Collapsing just inside the door
Billy (the bar owner)
Still talks about it to this day
'Remember that night you got so drunk
We had to carry you out of here?
I've never seen you like that'
Yeah, Billy
I've never seen me like that, either
It's probably a good thing
I don't remember most of that night

a writer

I fancy myself a writer
Although I rarely sit and write
Anything worth while
It's mostly short snippets of ideas
That I need to get out of my head
With the promise of coming back
And turning them into something
At a later date
I have a whole folder of
Ideas and snippets
Collected over the years
That haven't been turned into anything more
Than a few lines scribbled down
In the moment

I fancy myself a writer
But I can't really say I
Have much to show for it
Two so-called novels
Which are in a permanent state of revision
And various stories no where near ready
To be read by others
All with the same promise of
Getting them finished
And sharing them with someone else

But still
I fancy myself a writer
Because even if nothing is finished
And I have nothing published to show for it
I write

pavlov

Like Pavlov's dog
I salivate
At the mere mention
Of your name
But you'll never know that
I play it cool
Collected
Aloof
I hold my cards tightly to my chest and
Put on my best poker face
As I make a comment
Meant to be construed in many different ways
I just hope you pick the right one
So I don't have to show my hand
Or have you call my bluff

just dinner

The wheels are in motion
And there's no turning back
I'm okay with that
I think
As I climb into the passenger seat
Of your car
And we head down the road
I made the right decision
I'm pretty sure of that
It's just dinner, after all
Of course
I believe that as much
As I believe pigs can fly
But I'm not about to back out now

snap

My patience is all but worn thin
And something's got to give
Sooner or later
Because I don't know how much longer
I'll be able to tread water
And keep my head above the surface
It's all about survival
And I'm out to save myself
I learned long ago
That I can't save you
If you don't want to be saved
And I'm sorry you feel that way
Cuz you're a nice guy
When you're not being a jerk
But the worse the problem gets
The less and less I remember that nice guy
Even when he is around

apologies

I'm sorry
You don't understand how I feel
You can't comprehend what goes on in my head
You can't figure out why I'm not happy
You can't see the problem

I'm sorry
I'm not who you thought I'd be
I'm not trying hard enough
I'm not enough

I'm sorry
Things aren't the way we thought they'd be

right thing

No matter how much you try
To do the right thing
You're still doing the wrong thing to somebody
I suppose there's a way of balancing such things
But it's an art I have yet to master
So I try to do what'll piss off the
Least amount of people
And hope they'll understand

time

The clock slowly ticks down
The remaining minutes
Of another day
Another day full of possibilities
And wonder
And all of the things you were supposed to
Do today and didn't

if i...

If we can create our own happiness
Then I suppose
We can create our own sadness
And maybe it's just all in my head
Sitting here thinking
If I only did this
Or if I didn't do that
If I had this, not that
If I...
If I...
If I...

midnight

This last little drabble
Is only here
So I can say
I wrote right up
Until midnight tonight
Not wasting a minute
Except for all of the wasted minutes
From earlier in the day
But who's counting those?

I still have two more minutes
To use to my advantage
And make this poem
As rambling as can be
But I suppose that's what
Poetry is really
Some people are just better than others
When it comes to turning
A ramble into art
I don't think I'm one of those people though

So forgive this
Little collection of words
That might not even make sense
I'm just trying to use my time wisely
Or as wisely as I can

you

I don't know what it is about you
And why you affect me so
Or how you get under my skin
Like you do
You must have waved you magic wand
And instantly I was under your spell

left off

I'm worried about what happens
When you finally come back home
In this time apart
We both have done some soul searching
Growing as individuals
Moving on with our separate lives
In new directions
But soon our paths will converge
Once again
And I'm curious to see
If we can pick right up
Where we left off
Or if we'll have to get
Reacquainted with each other
All over again

monkey poetry

monkey

The monkey
Wakes me up
And tells me a joke

~*~*~*~

more monkey

The monkey
Reads a book
On a sunny day

~*~*~*~*~

still more monkey

The monkey
Runs fast
All day long

monkey writes a poem

The monkey laughs
And says
'I can write poetry, too'
I say
'Go right ahead'
And he hands me
a piece of paper that reads:

I love bananas
Bananas love me
We sit and enjoy the summer
In the banana tree

I read it
And begin to think
That the monkey
Is mocking me

sharing a home

It's hard sharing a home
With an alcoholic
Sharing someone you love and care about
With whiskey
It's hard for me
Even harder for my son
Who doesn't understand
What's going on around here
Of course, he's young enough
Where it indirectly affects him
Although I know from experience
It's affecting him
He'll only know that when he's older
I try to do my best
Try to keep this a stable household
But it's hard when you feel like
A single parent
In a two-parent household
I've tried to do whatever I can
To remedy the situation
But you can't help someone
Who doesn't want help

anticipation

It's the anticipation
That kills me
Can't get too excited
In case the whole thing
Falls apart
But can't talk yourself
Out of it either
In case it does work out

frame by frame

I move through life
One frame at a time
Stopping every so often
To check the script
Make sure I remember my lines
And where
I'm supposed to be standing
Waiting for a fade out
Or end scene

morning

It was one of those mornings
Perfect in the way the summer sun
Teased just enough light
Through the bedroom window
And lit up the room
Like your smile

And I smile
Taking in this perfect morning
In the sanctuary of the bedroom
On a Sunday
I peek out the window
Squinting from the bright light

Your touch is feather light
And I smile
As I look out the window
And the stillness of the morning
And the warmth of the sun
That shines into the room

The stillness of the room
Bathed in daylight
The warmth of the sun
And the joy of your smile
Another lazy morning
Spent looking out the window

I close the curtains on the window
Turning back towards the room
As end slowly comes to the morning
My source of light
Is your smile
As bright as the sun

You are the sunshine
That cascades through my window
You turn to me and smile
As you walk across the room
Dancing between the shadows and light
I wish you could be here every morning

It is long past morning and the sun
Is no longer shedding its light through the window
Leaving the room, I smile

middle of a dream

I was in the middle of a dream
Living in the moment
And I knew exactly how to feel
When you whispered
To me in the dark of night
Of things I could only imagine

There's a fine line between imagining
And dreaming
Your way through the night
Taking in the moment
Holding on to every whisper
And keeping close the feeling

It's the way you make me feel
Better than I could ever imagine
When you share in a whisper
All of your dreams
And I live in the moment
Of tonight

When morning takes over the night
These feelings
And this moment
That I could only imagine
Will become a dream
I can only hear my name being whispered

Just one more whisper
To end the night
Before I wake from my dream
And forget to feel
And try not to imagine
If only for a moment

I'm lost in this moment
With sweet words whispered
Leaving me to my imagination
And the dark of night
I wish I could feel
The way you make me feel in my dreams

Somewhere between a sweet dream and a never ending moment
You ask how I feel and I can only manage a whisper
I'm left to the night and my imagination

what was

Do you remember the last time we went to a bar?
We got raucously drunk
Spent the whole night laughing
And acting like a couple of fools?
We convinced ourselves we were still young
And wild

We're still wild
Although we've stopped going to bars
And we've surpassed the years of being young
And we've stopped getting drunk
But we still act like fools
And I can always make you laugh

And you can still make me laugh
As you run around wild
And acting a fool
Getting kicked out of some bar
Because you were drunk
And that girl was a bit too young

Youth is wasted on the young
You say with a laugh
Still a bit drunk
But you're always wild
In or out of a bar
And more and more I play your fool

But I refuse to play the role of the fool
Although I may still be trying to reclaim my youth
Now I do it outside of the bars
And I can't help but to laugh
About the two of us running wild
Like two raucous drunks

We've learned we don't need to be drunk
To act like fools
And run around wild
Even if we're no longer young
We can still share quite a few laughs
As we walk past the bars

We sit and reminisce about time spent in bars and getting drunk
Although we'll always laugh a bit too loud and act like fools
Cuz in our hearts, we're still young and wild

writing to find

I'm writing to find love
No,
Not that kind of love
The kind of love
Acceptance
Acknowledgment
Adoration
One can only get
From a jury of their
Writing peers
To be put on that
Imaginary list of
Must read
Must check out
I recommend
Authors

I'm writing to find myself
My own voice
My own niche
My own way
To dig down deep
And explore my soul
My heart
My mind

said it better

No matter how well
You try and phrase things
Somebody's already said it
And said it better
You can paraphrase
Borrow an idea
And even change the words around
But somebody's already said it
And said it better
Better than you
Could ever dream
Of saying it

great poetry reading day

According to my
Bizarre American holidays calendar
Today is
Great Poetry Reading Day
So I suggest going out
And finding a great poem to read
Not this one though

I suggest
Oh hell, anybody
(Although I'm partial to Bukowski)
But to each their own
So find a poet and
Pick a poem
And read it
(Even if you don't think it's
All that great when you've finished reading)
Except for this poem
Since it's neither great nor a poem really
It's just a really long
Run-on sentence
If you think about it…

your heartbeat

I don't know what it is
But I look forward to
Every night I get
To spend with you
Even if it feels too
Few and far between sometimes
I get the best night's sleep
Curled up in your arms
You're frame curled around mine
I lay there
Listening to your heartbeat
Listening to you breathe
The slow steady rhythm
Lulling me to sleep

I go back home
And it takes me a night or two to adjust
To my empty bed
And my silent room
Void of the sound of
Your heartbeat

deal

What to do
What to write
What to say
How to feel
About anyone
And anything
Anymore
There's always going to be someone
Who's waiting to jump
Waiting to attack
Waiting to take offense
Or waiting to read too much
Into things
But that's the risk you take
When you put your words
And thoughts
And feelings
Out there
On a public forum
If I thought about
All the people
I may or may not piss off
With anything I write
I wouldn't ever take the chance
But I don't have time
To sit and think
And try to read your mind
So I just write
How I feel
And if you don't like it
Deal

something with you

Make of this what you will
Because I'm tired of caring
And if you don't like it
That's your problem
I'm all done with
Putting my shit aside
To help you deal with yours
It's always something with you
Isn't it?
And I'm always there
With a supportive ear to listen with
A shoulder to cry on
Or whatever it is you need
And while I listen to you
Rant and rave
It makes me think my problems are
All in my head
And I need to grow the fuck up
And learn to deal
And that's what I do
I keep quiet
And it builds up inside
Because who wants to listen to
A stay-at-home mom
Bitch about her day?
It's not like she has to
Get up and deal with work problems
She's not in school
So she doesn't understand
Trying to balance homework and
A 9-to-5
She's married
So what does she know about
How horrible it is to
Find a date
Yeah, I never had to deal with any of that before
First of all
You get paid for your job

When your shift is over, you go home
And I have no idea what it's like
To balance school and a job
Waiting tables while in college doesn't count
And let's not get started
On the storybook ideal
Of happily married
Just because I have a husband
Doesn't mean it was easy for me
To find him
So I have no idea what the dating world is like
I listen to everyone else
Talk about how hard it is to be them
And I stay quiet
Because what the hell do I know
Right?

day of the year

It's coming up on that time of the year
Where I have to lower my expectations
And try not to put
Too much faith
Into those around me
All to make sure
I'm not let down
Because why should I expect
Some grand gesture on one day of the year
Not even a grand gesture
I'm not even expecting a mediocre gesture
It's easier that way
Because that way if someone
For some reason
Does do something
I can be genuinely surprised
And touched by their actions
I refuse to remind people
And guilt them into doing something
Just because of the date on the calendar
If they truly care
They'll remember on their own
And take it upon themselves
To do something nice
And if they don't
I'll still remember them on
Their one day of the year
Because that's the type of friend
That I am

i remember

There's that split second between
'Hey, how have you been?'
And
Kissing you
Where I wonder
'What the hell am I doing?'
You're so out of my league
And then you look up at me
And smile
And I remember
Exactly what I'm doing

bitch

I'm a raging bitch today
For whatever reason
Maybe it's because I could
Use a damn break
Maybe it's because I
Seem to be the only one
Who gives a damn around here
I'd like to see what would happen
If I went on strike
For a day
And you all had to fend for yourselves

turn back time

If I could turn back time
And take back
Every mistake we made
Every angry word we said
I still don't think
We'd be together now
We had a good run
But all good things
Must come to an end
At some point

get lost

I wish I could tell you
Just how easy it is for me
To get lost
In those brown eyes
Especially when you're smiling
All they show is love

It didn't take much for me to fall in love
With you
And the particular smile
Reserved only for me
And every time I look into your brown eyes
I still get lost

And I'm not sure what I'd do if I lost
You and your love
And I couldn't lose myself in those eyes
And I couldn't share my life with you
And you weren't here next to me
I'd no longer have a reason to smile

But I have a reason to smile
And not feel so lost
Because you're still here with me
And I'm in love
With you
And those brown eyes

Those brown eyes
The sparkle when you smile
And I fall deeper into you
Gladly getting lost
In the love
You have for me

And only me
It's those brown eyes
Showing nothing but love
That makes me smile
I could spend hours getting lost
In all of the things I love about you

Just a small glimpse into you and me
And getting lost in your beautiful brown eyes
And how I smile, completely in love

it's the way

It's the way
Your skin feels beneath
My fingertips
The shivers those light touches
Send dancing down your spine
It's the way
Your breath catches
In the middle of
Calling out my name
Like I actually
Took your breath away
It's the way
You cast your gaze
Down upon me
As I make my descent
And rest my head
On your broad chest
And you wrap your
Arms around me
It's the way
This moment is perfect
In its simplicity
Of you and me

fact or fiction

You can sit right there
And lie to my face
If it makes you feel better
About your lot in life
Cuz I already believe
What I choose to anyway
Whether you're telling me
Fact or fiction
It doesn't really matter
Because no one ever truly
Gives the one-hundred percent
Honest account
Of something that's happened
To them
We all embellish in
Some way
Shape
Or form
Something as simple as
Moving a decimal point
In your gross income
Or the oh-so-clever
Push-up bra
We all do it in some way
And you can either be
Naïve
And take things at their
Face value
Or you can be a
Cynic
And believe nothing
But I like to think somewhere in there
Lies a happy medium
The naïve cynic, maybe?
You can fool some of the people
Half of the time
And the rest never
Really cared anyway

tuck and roll

C'mon girl
Snap out of it
Move on
And let it go
Are you afraid of
Losing yourself
Losing all you've ever known
Jumping off the high dive
Into the unknown
Just make sure you
Tuck your head in
On the way down

a toast

Here's a toast
To all of those
Who have passed
Through these trying times
Before us
To their struggles
Their grief
Their pain
Their stride and gains
And losses
And all of the things
Miniscule or
Monumental
That allow us all of
The things we
Have now
Whether we are
Entitled to them
Or not
Because I'm sure the
Good fights which were
Fought
Were on the basis
Of your
Entitlement

rules

Who made up these rules
Of what is right
And what is wrong
Anyway?
And how many times have these rules
As they've been passed down
Through time
Been reinterpreted or misconstrued?
Who's to say what's
Right or wrong now
Was right or wrong then?
And in ten
Twenty
One hundred years from now
Will everything be turned
Upside down
Our wrongs will be rights
And our rights will all
Be wrong

free form

It's time again
For one of those
Nonsensical
Free form poems
That just seems to go
On and on
And never really make a point
It's only existence
Being a boost to my
Word count

But I kind of think
That's the beauty of
The poetic form
You can just write
And not worry about
Making sense of it all
It's freeing
Getting random ideas
Out of my head
And down on paper
(or on the screen, as it were)
And just letting it all out
Like a creative
Primal scream
Of some sort

And even if you write
With a specific idea in mind
Any number of readers will
Take from it what they see

I learned that lesson in college
In my creative writing class
As one of my poems was dissected
by the whole class
And one student turned to me
And read much more into my poem

Than I even realized was in there
To begin with
About my subconscious and my psyche
And how cleverly I masked
The true feelings behind it
And all I could think was
'It's just a poem'

call me baby

You call me baby
And I still blush
At the intimacy
That word conveys
Even after two years
Of hearing it
I still go weak
When you smile at me
In just the right way
And kisses exchanged
In stolen moments
Still send me floating
I guess it's a good thing
That after two years
You still effect me
The way you do

ker-plooey

You can only
Keep everything
Bottled up inside
Before you break open
And it all comes
Pouring out
Of your soul
At dangerous speeds
And when you're done
Firing off
Your loaded rounds
You'll be lucky
If anyone around you
Is left standing

dancers

It's like a very carefully choreographed
Dance we've been learning
You and I
The only trick to it
Is that
We're dancing in
Different rooms
Each to a
Different song

crossroads

The tides come and go
Shifting and settling
And I feel as if
I'm on the cusp
Of something more
Something tangible
Something surreal
A slow build
Crescendo
Building towards a great climax
As you stand at the crossroads
Go left?
Go right?
Whichever path you choose
Will forever change your life
No second chances
No looking back
Just moving forward to something more
Something real
Something great you've never seen before

always the way

If I could just…
Isn't that always the way, though
A world full of if only
And what if
And maybe

~~*~*

had to do

I hope you know
That walking away from you
Wasn't easy
But it was something
I had to do

~~*~*~*

rain

The wind blows colder
Gray clouds cover the blue sky
Signaling the rain

~~*~*

ideal standards

I feel like you're
Constantly judging me
Seeing if I
Measure up
To whatever ideal standard
You hold

second chance

You are my second chance
To make a first impression
To do things right
This time around

~~*~*~*

unfinished

It's a fine line
And I'm having a fine time
Dancing between
What is
And what should never be

~~*~*~*

trust

I place my trust
In the wrong people
But still end up
Surprised
When I get burned

~~*~*~*

regret

I regret nothing
Except maybe that one time
That one thing
But there's always an exception
To the rule, right?

in bed

You smile at me
As we are laying in bed
And I am at peace

~~*~*

where you've been

You walk into the room
and I'm immediately struck
By the scent of your cologne
Mixed with his
And I know just where you've been

www.ingramcontent.com/pod-product-compliance
Lightning Source LLC
Chambersburg PA
CBHW020010050426
42450CB00005B/392